Ireland

photographs by Tom Kelly

2001 ENGAGEMENT CALENDAR

Catalog No. 201212
Published by Pomegranate Communications, Inc., Box 6099, Rohnert Park, California 94927
© 2000 Tom Kelly

Available in the U.K. and mainland Europe from Pomegranate Europe Ltd.,
Fullbridge House, Fullbridge, Maldon, Essex CM9 4LE, England
Available in Australia from Boobook Publications Pty. Ltd.,
P.O. Box 163 or Freepost 1, Tea Gardens, NSW 2324
Available in New Zealand from Randy Horwood Ltd., P.O. Box 32-077, Devonport, Auckland
Available in Asia (including the Middle East), Africa, and Latin America from
Pomegranate International Sales, 113 Babcombe Drive, Thornhill, Ontario L3T 1M9, Canada

Pomegranate also publishes a 2001 wall calendar featuring Tom Kelly's photographs of Ireland, as well as a book of postcards, boxed notes, notecards, bookmarks, magnets, and an address book. Also available are many other calendars in various formats, as well as notecards, notecard folios and boxed notecard sets, art magnets, postcards and books of postcards, journals, books of days, address books, posters, bookmarks, Knowledge Cards™, mousepads, screensavers, and books. For more information, contact Pomegranate Communications, Inc.:
800-227-1428; www.pomegranate.com.

Front cover image: West County Cork
Back cover image: Country postbox, County Kerry

Cover design by Barbara Derringer

All astronomical data supplied in this calendar are expressed in Greenwich Mean Time (GMT).
Moon phases and American, Canadian, and U.K. holidays are noted.

● NEW MOON   ☽ FIRST QUARTER   ○ FULL MOON   ☾ LAST QUARTER

january

NEW YEAR'S DAY

monday

1 | 1

BANK HOLIDAY (SCOTLAND)

tuesday

☽ 2 | 2

When will that day-star,
   mildly springing,
Warm our isle with peace and love?
When will heaven,
   its sweet bell ringing,
Call my spirit to the fields above?

—THOMAS MOORE,
THE SONG OF FIONNUALA

wednesday

3 | 3

thursday

4 | 4

friday

5 | 5

seat of the high kings,
tara, county meath

saturday

6 | 6

S	M	T	W	T	F	S
	1	2	3	4	5	6
7	8	9	10	11	12	13
14	15	16	17	18	19	20
21	22	23	24	25	26	27
28	29	30	31			

january

sunday

7 | 7

january

monday
8 | 8

tuesday
○ **9** | 9

Sea-horses glisten in summer
Far as the glance of Bran
But streams of honey pour
Through the land of Manannan.

—THE DOUBLE VISION OF MANANNAN
(TRANS. JOHN MONTAGUE)

wednesday
10 | 10

thursday
11 | 11

friday
12 | 12

phoenix park, dublin

saturday
13 | 13

sunday
14 | 14

S	M	T	W	T	F	S
	1	2	3	4	5	6
7	8	9	10	11	12	13
14	15	16	17	18	19	20
21	22	23	24	25	26	27
28	29	30	31			

january

january

MARTIN LUTHER KING JR. DAY	*monday* 15
	tuesday ☾ 16

No storm has overthrown

The royal standing stone.

Every year the fertile plain

Bears its crop of yellow grain.

—THE HAG OF BEARE
(TRANS. JOHN MONTAGUE)

	wednesday 17
	thursday 18
	friday 19

Lough Allen,
County Leitrim

S	M	T	W	T	F	S
	1	2	3	4	5	6
7	8	9	10	11	12	13
14	15	16	17	18	19	20
21	22	23	24	25	26	27
28	29	30	31			

january

	saturday 20
	sunday 21

january

*I have loved the land of Ireland
almost beyond speech;
to sleep at Comgall's, to visit Canice,
it would be pleasant!*

—COLMCILLE (TRANS. JOHN MONTAGUE)

snowy hills,
county mayo

S	M	T	W	T	F	S
	1	2	3	4	5	6
7	8	9	10	11	12	13
14	15	16	17	18	19	20
21	22	23	24	25	26	27
28	29	30	31			

january

monday
22

tuesday
23

wednesday
● 24

thursday
25

friday
26

saturday
27

sunday
28

jan/feb

Who were the builders?
  Question not the silence

That settles on the lake
  for evermore,

Save when the sea-bird screams
  and to the islands

The echo answers from
  the steep-cliffed shore.

—WILLIAM LARMINIE, NAMELESS DOON

Royal Tara,
County Meath

S	M	T	W	T	F	S
				1	2	3
4	5	6	7	8	9	10
11	12	13	14	15	16	17
18	19	20	21	22	23	24
25	26	27	28			

february

monday
29 | 29

tuesday
30 | 30

wednesday
31 | 31

thursday
☽ **1** | 32

friday
2 | 33

saturday
3 | 34

sunday
4 | 35

february

monday
5 | 36

tuesday
6 | 37

Our rocks are rough, but smiling there
The acacia waves her yellow hair,
Lonely and sweet, nor loved the less
For flowering in a wilderness.
—THOMAS MOORE, *LALLA ROOKH*

wednesday
7 | 38

thursday
○ 8 | 39

friday
9 | 40

Glencolumbkille, County Donegal

saturday
10 | 41

S	M	T	W	T	F	S
				1	2	3
4	5	6	7	8	9	10
11	12	13	14	15	16	17
18	19	20	21	22	23	24
25	26	27	28			

february

sunday
11 | 42

february

LINCOLN'S BIRTHDAY

monday

12

tuesday

13

I found in Ulster,
    from hill to glen,

Hardy warriors, resolute men;

Beauty that bloomed
    when youth was gone,

And strength transmitted
    from sire to son.

    —PRINCE ALFRID'S ITINERARY
(TRANS. JAMES CLARENCE MANGAN)

VALENTINE'S DAY

wednesday

14

thursday

☾15

friday

16

Killala, County Mayo

saturday

17

S	M	T	W	T	F	S
				1	2	3
4	5	6	7	8	9	10
11	12	13	14	15	16	17
18	19	20	21	22	23	24
25	26	27	28			

february

sunday

18

february

PRESIDENTS' DAY

monday
19 | 50

tuesday
20 | 51

A hedge before me, one behind,
a blackbird sings from that,
above my small book many-lined
I apprehend his chat.

wednesday
21 | 52

Up trees, in costumes buff,
mild accurate cuckoos bleat,
Lord love me, good the stuff
I write in a shady seat.

—THE MONASTIC SCRIBE
(TRANS. FLANN O'BRIEN)

WASHINGTON'S BIRTHDAY

thursday
22 | 53

friday
● 23 | 54

Tralee, County Kerry

saturday
24 | 55

sunday
25 | 56

S	M	T	W	T	F	S
				1	2	3
4	5	6	7	8	9	10
11	12	13	14	15	16	17
18	19	20	21	22	23	24
25	26	27	28			

february

feb/mar

Amid the throng she passed along the meadow-floor:

Spring seemed to smile on Earth awhile, and then no more.

—JAMES CLARENCE MANGAN,
AND THEN NO MORE

Lake Derravaragh, County Westmeath

S	M	T	W	T	F	S
				1	2	3
4	5	6	7	8	9	10
11	12	13	14	15	16	17
18	19	20	21	22	23	24
25	26	27	28	29	30	31

march

monday
26 | 57

tuesday
27 | 58

ASH WEDNESDAY — *wednesday*
28 | 59

thursday
1 | 60

friday
2 | 61

saturday
☽ **3** | 62

sunday
4 | 63

march

monday
5 | 64

tuesday
6 | 65

*For music I
have pines, my tall
music-pines
so who can I
envy here, my
gentle Christ?*

— A HERMIT SPEAKS
(TRANS. MICHAEL HARTNETT)

wednesday
7 | 66

thursday
8 | 67

friday
○ 9 | 68

turf cutting, delphi,
county mayo

saturday
10 | 69

S	M	T	W	T	F	S
				1	2	3
4	5	6	7	8	9	10
11	12	13	14	15	16	17
18	19	20	21	22	23	24
25	26	27	28	29	30	31

march

sunday
11 | 70

march

monday
12 | 71

tuesday
13 | 72

Irishness is not primarily a question of birth or blood or language; it is the condition of being involved in the Irish situation, and usually of being mauled by it.

—CONOR CRUISE O'BRIEN

wednesday
14 | 73

thursday
15 | 74

friday
☾ 16 | 75

ST. PATRICK'S DAY

saturday
17 | 76

country postbox,
county kerry

S	M	T	W	T	F	S
				1	2	3
4	5	6	7	8	9	10
11	12	13	14	15	16	17
18	19	20	21	22	23	24
25	26	27	28	29	30	31

march

sunday
18 | 77

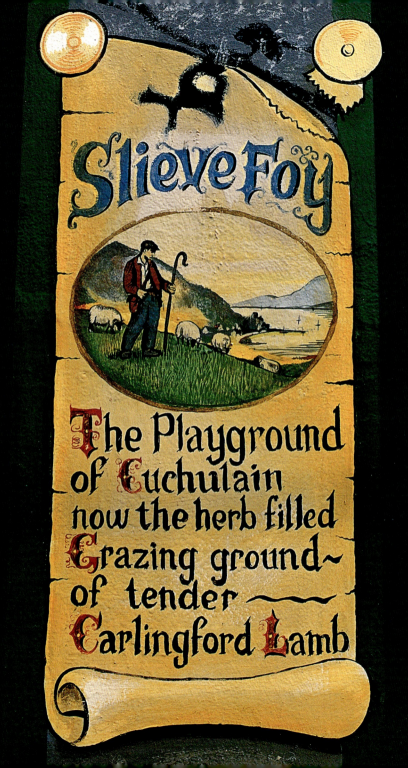

march

BANK HOLIDAY (N. IRELAND)

monday

19 | 78

VERNAL EQUINOX 1:31 P.M. (GMT)

tuesday

20 | 79

The ducks smooth-swimming
  the shining bay,

The swan all proud, to lead the way,

The blue of the lake and lusty wave,

Battering mad, in the gloomy cave.

—THE MIDNIGHT COURT
(TRANS. BRENDAN BEHAN)

wednesday

21 | 80

thursday

22 | 81

friday

23 | 82

carlingford,
county louth

saturday

24 | 83

S	M	T	W	T	F	S
				1	2	3
4	5	6	7	8	9	10
11	12	13	14	15	16	17
18	19	20	21	22	23	24
25	26	27	28	29	30	31

march

sunday

●25 | 84

mar/apr

monday
26 | 85

tuesday
27 | 86

wednesday
28 | 87

Fern clumps redden
shapes are hidden
wildgeese raise
wonted cries.

Cold now girds
wings of birds
icy time—
that's my rime.

—SCEL LEM DUIB
(TRANS. FLANN O'BRIEN)

thursday
29 | 88

friday
30 | 89

St. Finians, West Cork

saturday
31 | 90

S	M	T	W	T	F	S
	1	2	3	4	5	6	7
8	9	10	11	12	13	14
15	16	17	18	19	20	21
22	23	24	25	26	27	28
29	30					

april

DAYLIGHT SAVING TIME BEGINS

sunday
1 | 91

april

monday
2 | 92

tuesday
3 | 93

Lovely inlets of water,
sweet free running streams;
though tonight a spent veteran,
I lived in pleasant times.
— THE DESERTED MOUNTAIN
(TRANS. JOHN MONTAGUE)

wednesday
4 | 94

thursday
5 | 95

friday
6 | 96

FIRST NIGHT OF PASSOVER

moone high cross,
county kildare

saturday
7 | 97

S	M	T	W	T	F	S
	2	3	4	5	6	7
8	9	10	11	12	13	14
15	16	17	18	19	20	21
22	23	24	25	26	27	28
29	30					

PALM SUNDAY

sunday
○ 8 | 98

april

april

monday
9 | 99

tuesday
10 | 100

Hollybush, bar me
from winter winds.
Ash, be a spear
in my fearful hand.

wednesday
11 | 101

Birch, oh blessed
birchtree, sing
proudly the tangle
of the wind.

—HE PRAISES THE TREES
(TRANS. ROBIN SKELTON)

thursday
12 | 102

GOOD FRIDAY

friday
13 | 103

sligo, leitrim border

saturday
14 | 104

S	M	T	W	T	F	S
	1	2	3	4	5	6	7
8	9	10	11	12	13	14
15	16	17	18	19	20	21
22	23	24	25	26	27	28
29	30					

EASTER SUNDAY

sunday
☾ 15 | 105

april

april

EASTER MONDAY (CANADA, U.K.)

monday
16 | 106

tuesday
17 | 107

Over hills and through dales
Have I roamed for your sake;
All yesterday I sailed with sails
On river and on lake.
The Erne . . . at its highest flood
I dashed across unseen,
For there was lightning in my blood,
My Dark Rosaleen!
—DARK ROSALEEN
(TRANS. JAMES CLARENCE MANGAN)

wednesday
18 | 108

thursday
19 | 109

friday
20 | 110

County Wicklow

saturday
21 | 111

S	M	T	W	T	F	S
1	2	3	4	5	6	7
8	9	10	11	12	13	14
15	16	17	18	19	20	21
22	23	24	25	26	27	28
29	30					

april

EARTH DAY

sunday
22 | 112

april

monday
● 23

tuesday
24

> I heard a woman's voice that wailed
> Between the sandhills and the sea:
> The famished sea-bird past me sailed
> Into the dim infinity.
>
> —AUBREY DE VERE, *IN RUIN RECONCILED*

wednesday
25

thursday
26

friday
27

slane, county meath

saturday
28

S	M	T	W	T	F	S
1	2	3	4	5	6	7
8	9	10	11	12	13	14
15	16	17	18	19	20	21
22	23	24	25	26	27	28
29	30					

sunday
29

april

apr / may

Silent, O Moyle,
  be the roar of thy water,

Break not, ye breezes,
  your chain of repose,

While, murmuring mournfully,
  Lir's lonely daughter

Tells to the night-star
  her tale of woes.

—THOMAS MOORE,
THE SONG OF FIONNUALA

monday
☽ 30 | 120

tuesday
1 | 121

wednesday
2 | 122

thursday
3 | 123

friday
4 | 124

CINCO DE MAYO

saturday
5 | 125

sunday
6 | 126

mountains of mourne,
county louth

S	M	T	W	T	F	S
			1	2	3	4	5
6	7	8	9	10	11	12
13	14	15	16	17	18	19
20	21	22	23	24	25	26
27	28	29	30	31		

may

may

BANK HOLIDAY (U.K.)

monday
○ 7 | 127

tuesday
8 | 128

Roll forth, my song,
 like the rushing river
That sweeps along to the mighty sea;
God will inspire me while I deliver
My soul of thee!

—JAMES CLARENCE MANGAN,
THE NAMELESS ONE

wednesday
9 | 129

thursday
10 | 130

friday
11 | 131

Fethard,
County Tipperary

saturday
12 | 132

MOTHER'S DAY

sunday
13 | 133

S	M	T	W	T	F	S
		1	2	3	4	5
6	7	8	9	10	11	12
13	14	15	16	17	18	19
20	21	22	23	24	25	26
27	28	29	30	31		

may

may

monday
14 | 134

tuesday
☾ 15 | 135

And the belling of the stag
In Siodhmhuine's steep glen;
No music on earth soothes
My soul like its sweetness.

—SWEETNESS
(TRANS. JOHN MONTAGUE)

wednesday
16 | 136

thursday
17 | 137

friday
18 | 138

ARMED FORCES DAY

saturday
19 | 139

shoreline, galwag bag

S	M	T	W	T	F	S
		1	2	3	4	5
6	7	8	9	10	11	12
13	14	15	16	17	18	19
20	21	22	23	24	25	26
27	28	29	30	31		

m a g

sunday
20 | 140

may

VICTORIA DAY (CANADA)

monday
21 | 141

tuesday
22 | 142

The calm sea-level turns
 from white to rose;

And, as the space
 a richer glory grows,

The earliest bird sings
 faintly far away

Upon the poplar by the ocean steep.

—THOMAS CAULFIELD IRWIN,
WITH THE DAWN

wednesday
● 23 | 143

thursday
24 | 144

friday
25 | 145

painted window, cork

saturday
26 | 146

S	M	T	W	T	F	S
		1	2	3	4	5
6	7	8	9	10	11	12
13	14	15	16	17	18	19
20	21	22	23	24	25	26
27	28	29	30	31		

sunday
27 | 147

may/jun

MEMORIAL DAY OBSERVED
BANK HOLIDAY (U.K.)

monday
28

tuesday
☽ 29

When daffodils were altar gold
her lips were light on mine

And when the hawthorn was bright
we drank the new year's wine;

MEMORIAL DAY

wednesday
30

The nights seemed stained-glass
windows lit with love that
paled the sky,

But love's last ember perishes
in the winter of her eye.

—DONAGH MACDONAGH,
GOING TO MASS LAST SUNDAY

thursday
31

friday
1

Tree in field,
County Meath

saturday
2

S	M	T	W	T	F	S
					1	2
3	4	5	6	7	8	9
10	11	12	13	14	15	16
17	18	19	20	21	22	23
24	25	26	27	28	29	30

june

sunday
3

june

monday
4 | 155

tuesday
5 | 156

Small one, pathway
loiterer, green
leaved berry, give me
your speckled crimson.

wednesday
○ 6 | 157

Apple tree, let me
shake you strongly.
Rowan, drop me
your bright blossom.

—HE PRAISES THE TREES
(TRANS. ROBIN SKELTON)

thursday
7 | 158

friday
8 | 159

Botanical Gardens,
Dublin

saturday
9 | 160

S	M	T	W	T	F	S
					1	2
3	4	5	6	7	8	9
10	11	12	13	14	15	16
17	18	19	20	21	22	23
24	25	26	27	28	29	30

june

sunday
10 | 161

june

monday
18 | 169

tuesday
19 | 170

> The hedges are all drowned
>   in green grass seas,
>
> And bobbing poppies flare
>   like Elmo's light,
>
> While siren-like the
>   pollen-stained bees
>
> Drone in the clover depths.
>
> —FRANCIS LEDWIDGE, JUNE

wednesday
20 | 171

SUMMER SOLSTICE 7:38 A.M. (GMT)

thursday
● 21 | 172

friday
22 | 173

saturday
23 | 174

flowers
wellington boots

S	M	T	W	T	F	S
					1	2
3	4	5	6	7	8	9
10	11	12	13	14	15	16
17	18	19	20	21	22	23
24	25	26	27	28	29	30

june

sunday
24 | 175

jun/jul

monday 25 | 176

tuesday 26 | 177

A tune is more lasting than the voice of the birds,

A word is more lasting than the riches of the world.

—DOUGLAS HYDE,
LOVE SONGS OF CONNACHT

wednesday 27 | 178

thursday ☾ 28 | 179

friday 29 | 180

Kinvara, County Galway

saturday 30 | 181

S	M	T	W	T	F	S
	1	2	3	4	5	6	7
8	9	10	11	12	13	14
15	16	17	18	19	20	21
22	23	24	25	26	27	28
29	30	31				

july

CANADA DAY (CANADA)

sunday 1 | 182

july

CANADA DAY OBSERVED (CANADA)

monday

2 | 183

tuesday

3 | 184

*Fleeing from threatened flood,
   they sailed,*

*Seeking the fair island,
   without serpent or claw;*

INDEPENDENCE DAY

wednesday

4 | 185

*From the deck of their
   hasty barque watched*

*The soft edge of Ireland
   nearward draw.*

—THE FIRST INVASION OF IRELAND
(TRANS. JOHN MONTAGUE)

thursday

○ 5 | 186

friday

6 | 187

saturday

7 | 188

Ballintober,
County Mayo

S	M	T	W	T	F	S
1	2	3	4	5	6	7
8	9	10	11	12	13	14
15	16	17	18	19	20	21
22	23	24	25	26	27	28
29	30	31				

sunday

8 | 189

july

july

monday
9 | 190

tuesday
10 | 191

I demand a thatched house,
swept spick and span;
not a hut for dogs or cattle
but dignified in welcome:
I demand a high chair
cushioned with down.

—THE POET'S REQUEST
(TRANS. JOHN MONTAGUE)

wednesday
11 | 192

BANK HOLIDAY (N. IRELAND)

thursday
12 | 193

friday
13 | 194

Goughal, County Cork

saturday
14 | 195

S	M	T	W	T	F	S
1	2	3	4	5	6	7
8	9	10	11	12	13	14
15	16	17	18	19	20	21
22	23	24	25	26	27	28
29	30	31				

july

sunday
15 | 196

july

monday
16 | 197

tuesday
17 | 198

I found in Munster,
    unfettered of any,

Kings and queens,
    and poets a many—

Poets well skilled in music
    and measure,

Prosperous doings,
    mirth and pleasure.

—PRINCE ALFRID'S ITINERARY
(TRANS. JAMES CLARENCE MANGAN)

wednesday
18 | 199

thursday
19 | 200

friday
● 20 | 201

Deagh Castle,
County Limerick

saturday
21 | 202

S	M	T	W	T	F	S
	1	2	3	4	5	6	7
8	9	10	11	12	13	14
15	16	17	18	19	20	21
22	23	24	25	26	27	28
29	30	31				

july

sunday
22 | 203

july

monday
23 | 204

tuesday
24 | 205

The stags erupt from rivers,
brown mountains tell the distance:
I am glad as poor as this
even in men's absence.
—MARBAN, A HERMIT SPEAKS
(TRANS. MICHAEL HARTNETT)

wednesday
25 | 206

thursday
26 | 207

friday
☽ 27 | 208

county galway

saturday
28 | 209

S	M	T	W	T	F	S
	1	2	3	4	5	6	7
8	9	10	11	12	13	14
15	16	17	18	19	20	21
22	23	24	25	26	27	28
29	30	31				

july

sunday
29 | 210

jul/aug

monday 30 | 211

tuesday 31 | 212

The Silk of the Kine
shall rest at last;

What drove her forth
but the dragon-fly?

In the golden vale
she shall feed full fast,

With her mild gold horn
and her slow, dark eye.

—AUBREY DE VERE,
THE LITTLE BLACK ROSE

wednesday 1 | 213

thursday 2 | 214

friday 3 | 215

saturday ○ 4 | 216

Wicklow Gap,
County Wicklow

S	M	T	W	T	F	S
					1	2	3	4
5	6	7	8	9	10	11
12	13	14	15	16	17	18
19	20	21	22	23	24	25
26	27	28	29	30	31	

august

sunday 5 | 217

august

BANK HOLIDAY (SCOTLAND)

monday

6 | 218

tuesday

7 | 219

Hardly a mile from this pleasant clearing is a bright spring to drink from and use for moistening measured pieces of bread.

wednesday

8 | 220

For all my renouncing and sparse diet and regular tasks of reading and penance I foresee only delight in my days there.

—A HERMIT'S SONG
(TRANS. JAMES SIMMONS)

thursday

9 | 221

friday

10 | 222

cattle, county sligo

saturday

11 | 223

S	M	T	W	T	F	S
			1	2	3	4
5	6	7	8	9	10	11
12	13	14	15	16	17	18
19	20	21	22	23	24	25
26	27	28	29	30	31	

august

sunday

☾ 12 | 224

august

monday
13 | 225

tuesday
14 | 226

On some island I long to be,
a rocky promontory, looking on
the coiling surface of the sea.

wednesday
15 | 227

To see the waves, crest on crest
of the great shining ocean, composing
a hymn to the creator, without rest.

—COLMCILLE
(TRANS. JOHN MONTAGUE)

thursday
16 | 228

friday
17 | 229

Waterville,
County Kerry

saturday
18 | 230

sunday
● 19 | 231

S	M	T	W	T	F	S
			1	2	3	4
5	6	7	8	9	10	11
12	13	14	15	16	17	18
19	20	21	22	23	24	25
26	27	28	29	30	31	

august

august

monday
20

tuesday
21

Give thee safe passage
 on the wrinkled sea,

Himself thy pilot stand,

Bring thee through mist
 and foam to thy desire,

Again to Irish land.

—TO COLEMAN RETURNING
(TRANS. HELEN WADDELL)

wednesday
22

thursday
23

friday
24

saturday
☽ 25

west county cork

S	M	T	W	T	F	S
			1	2	3	4
5	6	7	8	9	10	11
12	13	14	15	16	17	18
19	20	21	22	23	24	25
26	27	28	29	30	31	

august

sunday
26

aug / sep

BANK HOLIDAY (U.K. EXCEPT SCOTLAND)

monday
27 | 239

tuesday
28 | 240

> The heron's lament by night,
> the moorhen in the heather—
> how sweet it was to hear
> their melodies twine together.
>
> —THE DESERTED MOUNTAIN
> (TRANS. JOHN MONTAGUE)

wednesday
29 | 241

thursday
30 | 242

friday
31 | 243

saturday
1 | 244

dunhill castle,
county waterford

S	M	T	W	T	F	S
						1
2	3	4	5	6	7	8
9	10	11	12	13	14	15
16	17	18	19	20	21	22
23	24	25	26	27	28	29
30						

september

sunday
2 | 245

september

ROSH HASHANAH (BEGINS AT SUNSET)

monday
● 17 | 260

tuesday
18 | 261

And age by age weak washing round the islands

No faintest sigh of story lisps the wave.

—WILLIAM LARMINIE,
THE NAMELESS DOON

wednesday
19 | 262

thursday
20 | 263

friday
21 | 264

AUTUMNAL EQUINOX 11:04 P.M. (GMT)

saturday
22 | 265

Yeats Sculpture,
Sligo Town

S	M	T	W	T	F	S
						1
2	3	4	5	6	7	8
9	10	11	12	13	14	15
16	17	18	19	20	21	22
23	24	25	26	27	28	29
30						

september

sunday
23 | 266

september

	monday
	☽ 24

	tuesday
	25

The stars stand up in the air
The sun and the moon are gone,
The strand of its waters is bare,
And her sway is swept from the swan.

    —THE STARS STAND UP IN THE AIR
    (TRANS. THOMAS MACDONAGH)

YOM KIPPUR (BEGINS AT SUNSET)

	wednesday
	26

	thursday
	27

	friday
	28

house, west cork

	saturday
	29

S	M	T	W	T	F	S
						1
2	3	4	5	6	7	8
9	10	11	12	13	14	15
16	17	18	19	20	21	22
23	24	25	26	27	28	29
30						

september

	sunday
	30

october

monday
1 | 274

tuesday
○ 2 | 275

A gipsy lit a fire and made a sound

Of moving tins,
   and from an oblong moon

The river seemed
   to gush across the ground

To the cracked metre
   of a marching tune.

—FRANCIS LEDWIDGE,
A TWILIGHT IN MIDDLE MARCH

wednesday
3 | 276

thursday
4 | 277

friday
5 | 278

knocknarea,
county sligo

saturday
6 | 279

sunday
7 | 280

S	M	T	W	T	F	S
	1	2	3	4	5	6
7	8	9	10	11	12	13
14	15	16	17	18	19	20
21	22	23	24	25	26	27
28	29	30	31			

october

october

COLUMBUS DAY OBSERVED
THANKSGIVING DAY (CANADA)

monday
8 | 281

tuesday
9 | 282

Warm, sweet streams water the earth,

And after the choicest of wine
  and mead,

Those fine and flawless people

Without sin, without guilt, couple.

—THE WOOING OF ETAIN

wednesday
☾ 10 | 283

thursday
11 | 284

COLUMBUS DAY

friday
12 | 285

muckross house,
killarney, county kerry

saturday
13 | 286

S	M	T	W	T	F	S
	1	2	3	4	5	6
7	8	9	10	11	12	13
14	15	16	17	18	19	20
21	22	23	24	25	26	27
28	29	30	31			

october

sunday
14 | 287

october

monday
15

tuesday
● 16

Sweet is the voice in the land of gold,
Sweet is the calling of the
   wild birds bold;
Sweet is the shriek of the heron hoar,
Sweet fall the billows of Bundatrore.
   —OISIN, *THINGS DELIGHTFUL*
   (TRANS. GEORGE SIGERSON)

wednesday
17

thursday
18

friday
19

dunmore castle,
limerick

saturday
20

S	M	T	W	T	F	S
	1	2	3	4	5	6
7	8	9	10	11	12	13
14	15	16	17	18	19	20
21	22	23	24	25	26	27
28	29	30	31			

sunday
21

october

monday
22

tuesday
23

Sing, Gile machree,
Sit down by me,
We now are joined
    and ne'er shall sever;
This hearth's our own,
Our hearts are one,
And peace is ours for ever!

—GERALD GRIFFIN, *GILE MACHREE*

UNITED NATIONS DAY

wednesday
☽ 24

thursday
25

friday
26

saturday
27

DAYLIGHT SAVING TIME ENDS

sunday
28

Wild flowers,
County Kerry

S	M	T	W	T	F	S
	1	2	3	4	5	6
7	8	9	10	11	12	13
14	15	16	17	18	19	20
21	22	23	24	25	26	27
28	29	30	31			

october

november

| | monday 5 | 309 |

| ELECTION DAY | tuesday 6 | 310 |

This one short hour pays lavishly back
For many a year of mourning;
I'd almost venture another flight,
There's so much joy in returning—
Watching out for the hallowed shore,
All other attractions scornin':
O Ireland! don't you hear me shout?
I bid you top of the mornin'.
— JOHN LOCKE, *THE EXILE'S RETURN, OR MORNING ON THE IRISH COAST*

| | wednesday 7 | 311 |

| | thursday ☾ 8 | 312 |

| | friday 9 | 313 |

Bailey Lighthouse, Dublin

| | saturday 10 | 314 |

| VETERANS DAY
REMEMBRANCE DAY (CANADA) | sunday 11 | 315 |

S	M	T	W	T	F	S
				1	2	3
4	5	6	7	8	9	10
11	12	13	14	15	16	17
18	19	20	21	22	23	24
25	26	27	28	29	30	

november

november

VETERANS DAY OBSERVED
REMEMBRANCE DAY OBSERVED (CANADA)

monday
12 | 316

tuesday
13 | 317

So simple is the earth we tread,
So quick with love and life her frame,
Ten thousand years have dawned
  and fled,
And still her magic is the same.

—STOPFORD A. BROOKE,
THE EARTH AND MAN

wednesday
14 | 318

thursday
●15 | 319

friday
16 | 320

wicklow mountains

saturday
17 | 321

S	M	T	W	T	F	S
				1	2	3
4	5	6	7	8	9	10
11	12	13	14	15	16	17
18	19	20	21	22	23	24
25	26	27	28	29	30	

november

sunday
18 | 322

november

monday
19 | 323

tuesday
20 | 324

In the sun, in her soil,
  in her station thrice blest,

With her back towards Britain,
  her face to the West,

Erin stands proudly insular
  on her steep shore,

And strikes her high harp 'mid
  the ocean's deep roar.

—WILLIAM DRENNAN, *ERIN*

wednesday
21 | 325

THANKSGIVING DAY

thursday
☽ 22 | 326

friday
23 | 327

Rossbeigh, County Kerry

saturday
24 | 32

S	M	T	W	T	F	S
				1	2	3
4	5	6	7	8	9	10
11	12	13	14	15	16	17
18	19	20	21	22	23	24
25	26	27	28	29	30	

november

sunday
25 | 329

nov/dec

monday 26 | 330

tuesday 27 | 331

*There is not in the wide world
  a valley so sweet*

*As that vale in whose bosom
  the bright waters meet;*

*O the last rays of feeling
  and life must depart,*

*Ere the bloom of that valley
  shall fade from my heart.*

—THOMAS MOORE,
THE MEETING OF THE WATERS

wednesday 28 | 332

thursday 29 | 333

friday ○ 30 | 334

Thatch Cottage Window

S	M	T	W	T	F	S
						1
2	3	4	5	6	7	8
9	10	11	12	13	14	15
16	17	18	19	20	21	22
23	24	25	26	27	28	29
30	31					

december

saturday 1 | 335

sunday 2 | 336

december

monday
3

tuesday
4

I know a valley fair,
Eileen aroon!
I knew a cottage there,
Eileen aroon!
Far in the valley's shade
I knew a gentle maid,
Flower of a hazel glade,
Eileen aroon!

—GERALD GRIFFIN,
EILEEN AROON (MY TREASURE)

wednesday
5

thursday
6

friday
☾ 7

Sunset and Tree,
County Wicklow

S	M	T	W	T	F	S
						1
2	3	4	5	6	7	8
9	10	11	12	13	14	15
16	17	18	19	20	21	22
23	24	25	26	27	28	29
30	31					

december

saturday
8

FIRST NIGHT OF HANUKKAH

sunday
9

december

monday
10 | 344

tuesday
11 | 345

It seemed to whisper "Quietness,"
Then quietly itself was gone:
Yet echoes of its mute caress
Were with me as the years went on.
—THE THREE COUNSELLORS

wednesday
12 | 346

thursday
13 | 347

friday
● **14** | 348

saturday
15 | 349

Kylemore Abbey,
County Galway

S	M	T	W	T	F	S
						1
2	3	4	5	6	7	8
9	10	11	12	13	14	15
16	17	18	19	20	21	22
23	24	25	26	27	28	29
30	31					

december

sunday
16 | 350

december

monday 17 | 351

tuesday 18 | 352

I'm weary for old Ireland
   —once again
To see her fields before me,
In sunshine or in rain!
And the longing in my heart
   when it comes o'er me
Stings like pain.
   —JOHN TODHUNTER, *LONGING*

wednesday 19 | 353

thursday 20 | 354

WINTER SOLSTICE 7:21 P.M. (GMT)

friday 21 | 355

murrisk, croagh patrick,
county mayo

saturday ☽ 22 | 356

S	M	T	W	T	F	S
						1
2	3	4	5	6	7	8
9	10	11	12	13	14	15
16	17	18	19	20	21	22
23	24	25	26	27	28	29
30	31					

december

sunday 23 | 357

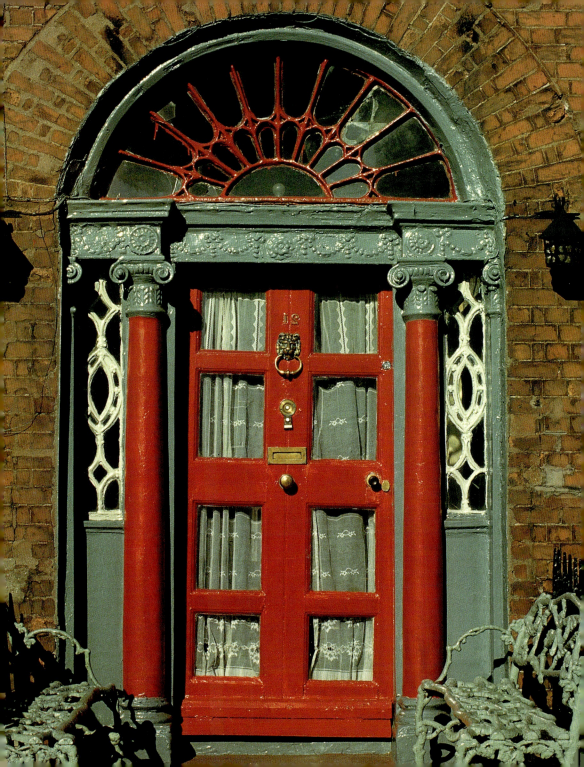

december

monday
24 | 358

CHRISTMAS DAY

tuesday
25 | 359

> When Erin first rose from
>   the dark swelling flood
>
> God bless'd the green Island,
>   and saw it was good;
>
> The em'rald of Europe,
>   it sparkled and shone—
>
> In the ring of the world
>   the most precious stone.
>
> —WILLIAM DRENNAN, *ERIN*

KWANZAA BEGINS
BOXING DAY (CANADA, U.K.)

wednesday
26 | 360

thursday
27 | 361

friday
28 | 362

dublin door

saturday
29 | 363

S	M	T	W	T	F	S
						1
2	3	4	5	6	7	8
9	10	11	12	13	14	15
16	17	18	19	20	21	22
23	24	25	26	27	28	29
30	31					

december

sunday
○ 30 | 364

dec/jan

monday
31 | 365

NEW YEAR'S DAY

tuesday
1 | 1

> When you are old and gray
>   and full of sleep,
>
> And nodding by the fire,
>   take down this book,
>
> And slowly read,
>   and dream of the soft look
>
> Your eyes had once,
>   and of their shadows deep.
>
>   —WILLIAM BUTLER YEATS,
>   WHEN YOU ARE OLD

BANK HOLIDAY (SCOTLAND)

wednesday
2 | 2

thursday
3 | 3

friday
4 | 4

Frosty Morning, County Meath

saturday
5 | 5

S	M	T	W	T	F	S
		1	2	3	4	5
6	7	8	9	10	11	12
13	14	15	16	17	18	19
20	21	22	23	24	25	26
27	28	29	30	31		

January

sunday
6 | 6

2001

JANUARY
S	M	T	W	T	F	S
	1	2	3	4	5	6
7	8	9	10	11	12	13
14	15	16	17	18	19	20
21	22	23	24	25	26	27
28	29	30	31			

MAY
S	M	T	W	T	F	S
		1	2	3	4	5
6	7	8	9	10	11	12
13	14	15	16	17	18	19
20	21	22	23	24	25	26
27	28	29	30	31		

SEPTEMBER
S	M	T	W	T	F	S
						1
2	3	4	5	6	7	8
9	10	11	12	13	14	15
16	17	18	19	20	21	22
23	24	25	26	27	28	29
30						

FEBRUARY
S	M	T	W	T	F	S
				1	2	3
4	5	6	7	8	9	10
11	12	13	14	15	16	17
18	19	20	21	22	23	24
25	26	27	28			

JUNE
S	M	T	W	T	F	S
					1	2
3	4	5	6	7	8	9
10	11	12	13	14	15	16
17	18	19	20	21	22	23
24	25	26	27	28	29	30

OCTOBER
S	M	T	W	T	F	S
	1	2	3	4	5	6
7	8	9	10	11	12	13
14	15	16	17	18	19	20
21	22	23	24	25	26	27
28	29	30	31			

MARCH
S	M	T	W	T	F	S
				1	2	3
4	5	6	7	8	9	10
11	12	13	14	15	16	17
18	19	20	21	22	23	24
25	26	27	28	29	30	31

JULY
S	M	T	W	T	F	S
1	2	3	4	5	6	7
8	9	10	11	12	13	14
15	16	17	18	19	20	21
22	23	24	25	26	27	28
29	30	31				

NOVEMBER
S	M	T	W	T	F	S
				1	2	3
4	5	6	7	8	9	10
11	12	13	14	15	16	17
18	19	20	21	22	23	24
25	26	27	28	29	30	

APRIL
S	M	T	W	T	F	S
1	2	3	4	5	6	7
8	9	10	11	12	13	14
15	16	17	18	19	20	21
22	23	24	25	26	27	28
29	30					

AUGUST
S	M	T	W	T	F	S
			1	2	3	4
5	6	7	8	9	10	11
12	13	14	15	16	17	18
19	20	21	22	23	24	25
26	27	28	29	30	31	

DECEMBER
S	M	T	W	T	F	S
						1
2	3	4	5	6	7	8
9	10	11	12	13	14	15
16	17	18	19	20	21	22
23	24	25	26	27	28	29
30	31					

2002

JANUARY
S	M	T	W	T	F	S
		1	2	3	4	5
6	7	8	9	10	11	12
13	14	15	16	17	18	19
20	21	22	23	24	25	26
27	28	29	30	31		

MAY
S	M	T	W	T	F	S
			1	2	3	4
5	6	7	8	9	10	11
12	13	14	15	16	17	18
19	20	21	22	23	24	25
26	27	28	29	30	31	

SEPTEMBER
S	M	T	W	T	F	S
1	2	3	4	5	6	7
8	9	10	11	12	13	14
15	16	17	18	19	20	21
22	23	24	25	26	27	28
29	30					

FEBRUARY
S	M	T	W	T	F	S
					1	2
3	4	5	6	7	8	9
10	11	12	13	14	15	16
17	18	19	20	21	22	23
24	25	26	27	28		

JUNE
S	M	T	W	T	F	S
						1
2	3	4	5	6	7	8
9	10	11	12	13	14	15
16	17	18	19	20	21	22
23	24	25	26	27	28	29
30						

OCTOBER
S	M	T	W	T	F	S
		1	2	3	4	5
6	7	8	9	10	11	12
13	14	15	16	17	18	19
20	21	22	23	24	25	26
27	28	29	30	31		

MARCH
S	M	T	W	T	F	S
					1	2
3	4	5	6	7	8	9
10	11	12	13	14	15	16
17	18	19	20	21	22	23
24	25	26	27	28	29	30
31						

JULY
S	M	T	W	T	F	S
	1	2	3	4	5	6
7	8	9	10	11	12	13
14	15	16	17	18	19	20
21	22	23	24	25	26	27
28	29	30	31			

NOVEMBER
S	M	T	W	T	F	S
					1	2
3	4	5	6	7	8	9
10	11	12	13	14	15	16
17	18	19	20	21	22	23
24	25	26	27	28	29	30

APRIL
S	M	T	W	T	F	S
	1	2	3	4	5	6
7	8	9	10	11	12	13
14	15	16	17	18	19	20
21	22	23	24	25	26	27
28	29	30				

AUGUST
S	M	T	W	T	F	S
				1	2	3
4	5	6	7	8	9	10
11	12	13	14	15	16	17
18	19	20	21	22	23	24
25	26	27	28	29	30	31

DECEMBER
S	M	T	W	T	F	S
1	2	3	4	5	6	7
8	9	10	11	12	13	14
15	16	17	18	19	20	21
22	23	24	25	26	27	28
29	30	31				

notes

notes